Great-Tasting
Potatoes

Publications International, Ltd.
www.pilcookbooks.com

Pictured on the front cover *(clockwise from top right):* Parmesan Potato Wedges *(page 54),* Roasted Peppers and Potatoes *(page 74),* Grilled Potato Salad *(page 90)* and Taco-Topped Potatoes *(page 76).*
Pictured on the back cover *(clockwise from top right):* Chunky Ranch Potatoes *(page 60),* Yankee Pot Roast and Vegetables *(page 30)* and Scalloped Potato-Onion Bake *(page 78).*

ISBN-13: 978-1-4127-2024-3
ISBN-10: 1-4127-2024-9

Manufactured in China.

8 7 6 5 4 3 2 1

Microwave Cooking: Microwave ovens vary in wattage. Use the cooking times as guidelines and check for doneness before adding more time.

Preparation/Cooking Times: Preparation times are based on the approximate amount of time required to assemble the recipe before cooking, baking, chilling or serving. These times include preparation steps such as measuring, chopping and mixing. The fact that some preparations and cooking can be done simultaneously is taken into account. Preparation of optional ingredients and serving suggestions is not included.

Publications International, Ltd.
www.pilcookbooks.com

Table of Contents

Spud Soups & Chowders

Bacon Potato Chowder

4 slices bacon
1 large onion, chopped (about 1 cup)
4 cans (10¾ ounces *each*) CAMPBELL'S® Condensed Cream of Potato Soup
4 soup cans milk
¼ teaspoon ground black pepper
2 large russet potatoes, cut into ½-inch pieces (about 3 cups)
2 cups shredded Cheddar cheese (8 ounces)
½ cup chopped fresh chives

1. Cook bacon in 6-quart saucepot over medium-high heat until it's crisp. Remove bacon with a fork and drain on paper towels. Crumble the bacon.

2. Add the onion and cook in the hot drippings until tender.

3. Stir the soup, milk, black pepper and potatoes into the saucepot. Heat to a boil. Reduce the heat to low. Cover and cook for 15 minutes or until the potatoes are tender. Remove from the heat.

4. Add the cheese and stir until the cheese melts. Serve with the chives.

Makes 8 servings

Prep: 15 minutes
Cook: 30 minutes

Transporting Tip: Transfer the chowder to a slow cooker. Chowder tends to thicken upon standing, so bring along some SWANSON® Vegetable or Chicken Broth to stir in before serving.

Chile Verde Chicken Stew

⅓ cup all-purpose flour
1½ teaspoons salt, divided
¼ teaspoon black pepper
1½ pounds boneless skinless chicken breasts, cut into 1½-inch chunks
4 tablespoons vegetable oil, divided
1 pound tomatillos (about 9), husked and halved
2 medium onions, chopped
2 cans (4 ounces each) mild green chiles
1 tablespoon dried oregano
1 tablespoon ground cumin
2 cloves garlic, chopped
1 teaspoon sugar
2 cups reduced-sodium chicken broth
8 ounces Mexican beer
5 red potatoes, diced
   Chopped fresh cilantro, sour cream, shredded Monterey Jack cheese, lime wedges, diced avocado and/or hot pepper sauce (optional)

1. Combine flour, 1 teaspoon salt and pepper in large bowl. Add chicken; toss to coat. Heat 2 tablespoons oil in large nonstick skillet over medium heat. Add chicken; cook until lightly browned on all sides. Transfer chicken to Dutch oven.

2. Heat remaining 2 tablespoons oil in same skillet. Stir in tomatillos, onions, green chiles, oregano, cumin, garlic, sugar and remaining ½ teaspoon salt. Cook over medium heat 20 minutes or until vegetables are softened, stirring frequently. Stir in broth and beer. Process mixture in batches in food processor or blender until almost smooth.

3. Add mixture to chicken in Dutch oven; stir in potatoes. Cover and bring to a boil over medium-high heat. Reduce heat to low; simmer, stirring occasionally, 1 hour or until potatoes are tender. Season to taste with salt and pepper.

4. Serve with desired toppings.

Makes 6 servings

Deep Bayou Chowder

            1 tablespoon olive oil
        1½ cups chopped onions
            1 large green bell pepper, chopped
            1 large carrot, chopped
            8 ounces red potatoes, diced
            1 cup frozen corn
            1 cup water
            ½ teaspoon dried thyme
            2 cups milk
            2 tablespoons chopped parsley
        1½ teaspoons seafood seasoning
            ¾ teaspoon salt

1. Heat oil in Dutch oven over medium-high heat. Add onions, pepper and carrot; cook and stir 4 minutes or until onions are translucent.

2. Add potatoes, corn, water and thyme; bring to a boil over high heat. Reduce heat; cover and simmer 15 minutes or until potatoes are tender. Stir in milk, parsley, seasoning and salt. Cook 5 minutes more.   *Makes 6 servings*

Rustic Vegetable Soup

        1 to 2 baking potatoes, cut into ½-inch pieces
        1 package (10 ounces) frozen mixed vegetables, thawed
        1 package (10 ounces) frozen cut green beans, thawed
        1 medium green bell pepper, chopped
        1 jar (16 ounces) picante sauce
        1 can (10 ounces) condensed beef broth, undiluted
        ½ teaspoon sugar
        ¼ cup finely chopped fresh parsley

Slow Cooker Directions
Combine all ingredients except parsley in slow cooker. Cover; cook on LOW 8 hours or on HIGH 4 hours. Stir in parsley.   *Makes 8 servings*

Potato & Spinach Soup with Gouda

        6 cups cubed peeled Yukon Gold potatoes (about 9 medium)
        2 cans (about 14 ounces each) chicken broth
        ½ cup water
        1 small red onion, finely chopped
        5 ounces baby spinach
        ½ teaspoon salt
        ¼ teaspoon ground red pepper
        ¼ teaspoon black pepper
    2½ cups shredded smoked Gouda cheese, divided
        1 can (12 ounces) evaporated milk
        1 tablespoon olive oil
        4 cloves garlic, cut into thin slices
        Chopped fresh parsley

Slow Cooker Directions

1. Combine potatoes, broth, water, onion, spinach, salt, red pepper and black pepper in slow cooker. Cover; cook on LOW 10 hours or on HIGH 4 to 5 hours.

2. *Turn slow cooker to HIGH.* Slightly mash potatoes in slow cooker; add 2 cups cheese and evaporated milk. Cover; cook on HIGH 15 to 20 minutes or until cheese is melted.

3. Heat oil in small skillet over low heat. Add garlic; cook and stir 2 minutes or until golden brown. Sprinkle soup with garlic, remaining ½ cup cheese and parsley.

Makes 8 to 10 servings

Pepper & Corn Cream Chowder

2 tablespoons butter
1 cup chopped onion
2 Anaheim chile peppers,* seeded and diced
½ cup thinly sliced celery
1 package (16 ounces) frozen corn
12 ounces unpeeled new red potatoes, diced
4 cups whole milk
6 ounces cream cheese, cubed
2 teaspoons salt
¾ teaspoon black pepper

*Mild, with just the hint of a bite, Anaheim chiles are medium green peppers with a long, narrow shape. Green bell peppers may be substituted.

1. Melt butter in large saucepan over medium-high heat. Add onion, Anaheim peppers and celery; cook and stir 5 minutes or until onion is translucent.

2. Add corn, potatoes and milk. Bring to a boil. Reduce heat to medium-low; cover and simmer 10 minutes or until potatoes are tender.

3. Remove from heat; add cream cheese, salt and black pepper. Stir until cream cheese is melted.   *Makes 4 to 6 servings*

Tater Tip

New potatoes are young potatoes. They may be any variety, but most often are round reds. New potatoes can be as small as marbles or almost as large as full-size potatoes, and they should have a very thin wispy skin. The sugar in these young potatoes has not completely converted to starch, so they have a crisp, waxy texture. In addition to being boiled and added to dishes such as soups, they are excellent in potato salad or roasted and eaten on their own.

Roasted Sweet Potato Soup

5 medium sweet potatoes (about 2 pounds)
2 tablespoons butter
1 medium onion, chopped (about 1 cup)
2 stalks celery, chopped (about 1 cup)
6 cups SWANSON® Chicken Broth (Regular, Natural Goodness™ or Certified Organic)
1 medium potato, peeled and cut into cubes (about 1 cup)
⅓ cup maple syrup
⅛ teaspoon ground white pepper
2 tablespoons light cream (optional)

1. Pierce the sweet potatoes with a fork. Microwave on HIGH for 8 to 13 minutes or bake at 400°F. for 1 hour or until they're fork-tender. Cut in half lengthwise. Scoop out sweet potato pulp and set aside.

2. Heat the butter in a 6-quart saucepot over medium heat. Add the onion and celery to the saucepot and cook until tender. Add the broth and potato. Heat to a boil. Reduce the heat to low. Cook for 15 minutes or until the potato is tender. Add the maple syrup, white pepper and reserved sweet potato.

3. Place ⅓ of the broth mixture into an electric blender or food processor container. Cover and blend until smooth. Pour the mixture into a large bowl. Repeat the blending process twice more with the remaining broth mixture. Return all of the puréed mixture to the saucepot. Add the cream, if desired. Cook over medium heat until the mixture is hot. Season to taste.

Makes 8 servings

Prep Time: 30 minutes
Cook Time: 20 minutes

Time-Saving Tip: Substitute 3¾ cups mashed, drained, canned sweet potatoes for the fresh sweet potatoes.

Potato Cheddar Soup

  2 pounds new red potatoes, cut into ½-inch cubes
¾ cup coarsely chopped carrots
  1 medium onion, coarsely chopped
  3 cups chicken broth
½ teaspoon salt
  1 cup half-and-half
¼ teaspoon black pepper
  2 cups (8 ounces) shredded Cheddar cheese

Slow Cooker Directions

1. Layer potatoes, carrots, onion, broth and salt in slow cooker. Cover; cook on LOW 6 to 7 hours or on HIGH 3 to 3½ hours or until vegetables are tender.

2. Stir in half-and-half and pepper. Cover; cook on HIGH 15 minutes. Turn off heat; let stand, uncovered, 5 minutes. Stir in cheese until melted. *Makes 6 servings*

Cream-Cheesy Garden Chowder

  1 can (about 14 ounces) chicken broth
  2 cups frozen corn
  2 cups frozen diced hash brown potatoes
  1 cup chopped green bell peppers
  1 teaspoon seafood seasoning
½ teaspoon dried thyme
⅛ teaspoon red pepper flakes (optional)
½ cup milk
  2 ounces cream cheese, cut into small pieces
¼ teaspoon salt
    Black pepper

1. Bring broth to a boil in large saucepan over high heat. Add corn, hash browns, bell peppers, seafood seasoning, thyme and red pepper, if desired. Return to a boil. Reduce heat to medium. Cover; simmer 15 minutes or until peppers are tender.

2. Remove from heat. Whisk in milk, cream cheese, salt and black pepper until cream cheese melts. Let stand 5 minutes before serving. *Makes 4 servings*

Blue Cheese Potato Soup
with Olive Tapenade

2 tablespoons olive oil
2 medium onions, chopped (about 1 cup)
5 cloves garlic, minced
6 cups SWANSON® Vegetable Broth (Regular *or* Certified Organic)
4 pounds red potatoes, peeled and diced
1 tablespoon balsamic vinegar
⅓ cup crumbled blue cheese
½ cup prepared olive tapenade

1. Heat the oil in a 6-quart saucepot over medium heat. Add the onions and garlic and cook until they're tender.

2. Stir the broth and potatoes in the saucepot and heat to a boil. Reduce the heat to low. Cover and cook for 30 minutes or until the potatoes are tender.

3. Pour ⅓ of the broth mixture into a blender or food processor. Cover and blend until smooth. Pour the mixture into a large bowl. Repeat twice more with the remaining broth mixture. Return all of the puréed mixture to the saucepot. Stir in the vinegar and cheese. Increase the heat to medium. Cook for 5 minutes or until the mixture is hot and bubbling. Season as desired.

4. Divide the soup mixture among **12** serving bowls. Top **each** with **2 teaspoons** tapenade.   *Makes 12 servings*

Prep Time: 20 minutes
Cook Time: 40 minutes

Kitchen Tip: Serve with a hot crusty French baguette. For dessert serve chocolate mousse pudding.

Meat & Potato Meals

Bratwurst Skillet Breakfast

1½ pounds red potatoes
3 bratwurst links (about ¾ pound)
2 tablespoons butter
1½ teaspoons caraway seeds
4 cups shredded red cabbage

1. Cut potatoes into ½-inch pieces. Place in microwavable baking dish. Microwave, covered, on HIGH 3 minutes; stir. Microwave 2 minutes more or just until tender.

2. Cut sausage into ¼-inch slices. Cook in large skillet over medium-high heat 8 minutes or until browned and cooked through. Transfer to paper towels. Pour off drippings.

3. Melt butter in same skillet. Add potatoes and caraway seeds. Cook, stirring occasionally, 6 to 8 minutes or until potatoes are golden and tender. Return sausage to skillet; stir in cabbage. Cook, covered, 3 minutes or until cabbage is slightly wilted. Uncover and stir 3 to 4 minutes or until cabbage is just tender.   *Makes 4 servings*

Prep and Cook Time: 30 minutes

Serving Suggestion: Serve with fresh fruit.

Ham, Poblano and Potato Casserole

¼ cup (½ stick) butter
¼ cup all-purpose flour
1½ cups whole milk
2 pounds baking potatoes, halved and thinly sliced
6 ounces thinly sliced ham, cut into bite-size pieces
1 poblano pepper, cut into thin strips (about 1 cup)
1 cup corn
1 cup chopped red bell pepper
1 cup finely chopped onion
1½ teaspoons salt
¼ teaspoon black pepper
¼ teaspoon ground nutmeg
1½ cups (6 ounces) shredded sharp Cheddar cheese

1. Preheat oven to 350°F. Spray 13×9-inch baking dish with nonstick cooking spray.

2. Melt butter in medium saucepan over medium heat. Add flour; whisk until smooth. Add milk; whisk until smooth. Cook and stir 5 to 7 minutes or until thickened. Remove from heat.

3. Layer one third of potatoes and half of ham, poblano pepper, corn, bell pepper and onion in prepared baking dish. Sprinkle with half of salt, pepper and nutmeg. Repeat layers. Top with remaining third of potatoes. Spoon white sauce evenly over all.

4. Cover with foil; bake 45 minutes. Uncover; bake 30 minutes more or until potatoes are tender. Sprinkle with cheese; bake 5 minutes or until cheese is melted. Let stand 15 minutes before serving.   *Makes 6 servings*

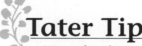

Tater Tip

Use a food processor with the slicing blade attachment, a v-slicer or a mandoline to thinly cut potatoes into perfectly even slices.

Chipotle Lamb Chops with Crispy Potatoes

4 lamb loin chops
2 teaspoons chipotle chili powder
   Salt and black pepper
8 ounces fingerling potatoes
2 tablespoons olive oil
   Olive oil cooking spray

1. Rub lamb chops with chili powder. Season with salt and pepper.

2. Cut potatoes into ¼-inch-thick slices. Heat oil in large nonstick skillet over medium heat. Add potatoes, stirring to coat with oil; season with salt and pepper. Cook 15 to 20 minutes or until golden brown and crispy, stirring occasionally.

3. Meanwhile, spray medium nonstick skillet with cooking spray. Add lamb chops. Cook 12 to 15 minutes or until medium rare (145°F), turning once. Serve lamb chops with potatoes.

Makes 2 servings

Ham and Sweet Potato Skillet

2 medium sweet potatoes (about 1¼ pounds)
3 cups water
1 tablespoon salt
1 fully cooked ham steak (about 1 pound)
½ cup brewed coffee
¼ cup pure maple syrup
2 tablespoons butter
½ cup coarsely chopped pecans, toasted*

*To toast pecans, place in nonstick skillet. Cook and stir over medium-low heat until pecans begin to brown, about 5 minutes. Remove immediately to plate to cool.

1. Peel sweet potatoes; cut into ¾-inch pieces. Combine water and salt in large saucepan over medium heat. Add sweet potatoes. Simmer 8 to 10 minutes or until almost tender; drain well.

2. Meanwhile, cut ham into ¾-inch chunks; discard bone and fat.

3. Combine coffee, maple syrup and butter in large skillet. Bring to a boil. Reduce heat; simmer 3 minutes. Add sweet potatoes and ham; simmer, stirring occasionally, until ham is hot and sauce is bubbly and slightly thickened. Sprinkle with pecans.

Makes 4 servings

Potato Sausage Casserole

        1 pound bulk pork sausage or ground pork
        1 can (10¾ ounces) condensed cream of mushroom soup, undiluted
        ¾ cup milk
        ½ cup chopped onion
        ½ teaspoon salt
        ¼ teaspoon black pepper
        3 cups sliced potatoes
        ½ tablespoon butter, cut into small pieces
     1½ cups (6 ounces) shredded Cheddar cheese
            Sliced green onions (optional)

1. Preheat oven to 350°F. Spray 1½-quart casserole with nonstick cooking spray.

2. Brown sausage in large skillet over medium heat, stirring to break up meat; drain fat.

3. Stir together soup, milk, onion, salt and pepper in medium bowl.

4. Place half of potatoes in prepared casserole. Top with half of soup mixture; top with half of sausage. Repeat layers, ending with sausage. Dot with butter.

5. Cover casserole with foil. Bake 1¼ to 1½ hours or until potatoes are tender. Uncover; sprinkle with cheese. Bake until cheese is melted and casserole is bubbly. Garnish with green onions.

Makes 6 servings

Tater Tip

Store potatoes in a cool, dark, well-ventilated place (light and warmth encourage sprouting) for up to two weeks. Check them occasionally and remove any that have sprouted or begun to shrivel. One rotten potato can spoil the whole lot. Avoid storing potatoes and onions together as the gases given off by the onions can cause the potatoes to spoil more quickly. Avoid storing potatoes in the refrigerator as the starch turns to sugar, making them overly sweet.

Yankee Pot Roast and Vegetables

1 beef chuck pot roast (2½ pounds)
  Salt and black pepper
3 medium baking potatoes, cut into quarters
2 large carrots, cut into ¾-inch slices
2 stalks celery, cut into ¾-inch slices
1 medium onion, sliced
1 large parsnip, cut into ¾-inch slices
2 bay leaves
1 teaspoon dried rosemary
½ teaspoon dried thyme
½ cup reduced-sodium beef broth

Slow Cooker Directions

1. Trim and discard excess fat from meat. Cut meat into ¾-inch pieces; sprinkle with salt and pepper.

2. Combine potatoes, carrots, celery, onion, parsnip, bay leaves, rosemary and thyme in slow cooker. Place beef over vegetables. Pour broth over beef. Cover; cook on LOW 8½ to 9 hours or until beef is fork-tender.

3. Remove and discard bay leaves. Transfer beef and vegetables to serving platter.

Makes 10 to 12 servings

Prep Time: 10 minutes
Cook Time: 8½ to 9 hours

Note: To make gravy, ladle the juices into a 2-cup measure; let stand 5 minutes. Skim off the fat. Measure the remaining juices and heat to a boil in a small saucepan. For each cup of juices, mix 2 tablespoons flour with ¼ cup cold water in a small bowl until smooth; add to the boiling juices. Cook and stir constantly 1 minute or until thickened.

Italian-Style Shepherd's Pie

1 pound potatoes, peeled and quartered
2 to 3 tablespoons reduced-sodium chicken broth
3 tablespoons grated Parmesan cheese
1 pound ground beef
½ cup chopped onion
2 teaspoons Italian seasoning
¼ teaspoon fennel seeds, crushed (optional)
⅛ teaspoon ground red pepper
2 cups sliced yellow summer squash
1 can (about 14 ounces) chunky pasta-style tomatoes, drained
1 cup frozen corn
⅓ cup tomato paste

1. Preheat oven to 375°F. Combine potatoes and enough water to cover in medium saucepan. Bring to a boil. Boil, uncovered, 20 to 25 minutes or until tender; drain. Mash potatoes, adding enough broth to reach desired consistency. Stir in Parmesan cheese.

2. Brown beef and onion in large skillet over medium-high heat 6 to 8 minutes, stirring to break up meat. Drain fat. Stir in Italian seasoning, fennel seeds, if desired, and red pepper. Add squash, tomatoes, corn and tomato paste; mix well. Spoon mixture into 2-quart casserole. Pipe or spoon potatoes over top.

3. Bake 20 to 25 minutes or until meat mixture is bubbly. Let stand 10 minutes before serving. *Makes 6 servings*

Chili Meatloaf and Potato Bake

1½ pounds ground turkey
¾ cup salsa
1 tablespoon chili powder
1 egg, beaten
1⅓ cups *French's*® French Fried Onions, divided
½ teaspoon salt
¼ teaspoon ground black pepper
2 cups prepared hot mashed potatoes
2 cups (8 ounces) shredded taco blend cheese, divided

1. Preheat oven to 375°F. Combine ground turkey, salsa, chili powder, egg, ⅔ cup French Fried Onions, salt and pepper until blended. Press turkey mixture into 9-inch square baking dish.

2. Bake 25 minutes or until turkey is cooked through and juices run clear. Drain off fat.

3. Combine potatoes and 1 cup cheese. Spread evenly over meatloaf. Sprinkle with remaining cheese and onions; bake 5 minutes or until cheese is melted and onions are golden.   *Makes 6 servings*

Prep Time: 15 minutes
Cook Time: 30 minutes

Tip: Prepare instant mashed potatoes for 4 servings.

Variation: For added Cheddar flavor, substitute *French's*® Cheddar French Fried Onions for the original flavor.

International Taters

Spanish Tapas Potatoes (Patatas Bravas)

2½ pounds small red potatoes, quartered
⅓ cup plus 2 tablespoons olive oil, divided
1 teaspoon coarse or kosher salt
½ teaspoon dried rosemary
1 can (about 14 ounces) diced tomatoes
2 tablespoons red wine vinegar
1 tablespoon minced garlic
1 tablespoon chili powder
1 tablespoon paprika
¼ teaspoon salt
¼ teaspoon chipotle chili powder
⅛ to ¼ teaspoon ground red pepper

1. Preheat oven to 425°F.

2. Combine potatoes, 2 tablespoons oil, coarse salt and rosemary in large bowl; toss to coat. Spread mixture in large shallow baking pan. Roast potatoes 35 to 40 minutes or until crisp and brown, turning every 10 minutes.

3. For sauce, combine tomatoes, remaining ⅓ cup oil, vinegar, garlic, chili powder, paprika, ¼ teaspoon salt, chipotle chili powder and red pepper in blender or food processor. Process just until blended. Transfer to large saucepan. Cover; cook over medium-high heat 5 minutes or until slightly thickened. Cool slightly.

4. To serve, drizzle sauce over potatoes or serve sauce in separate bowl for dipping.

Makes 10 to 12 servings

Note: Sauce can be made up to 24 hours ahead of time. Cover and refrigerate. Bring to room temperature or reheat before serving.

Spicy African Chickpea and Sweet Potato Stew

      Spice Paste (recipe follows)
1½ pounds sweet potatoes, peeled and cubed
  2 cups vegetable broth or water
  1 can (about 15 ounces) chickpeas, rinsed and drained
  1 can (about 14 ounces) diced tomatoes
1½ cups sliced fresh okra *or* 1 package (10 ounces) frozen cut okra, thawed
      Yellow Couscous (page 40)
      Hot pepper sauce
      Fresh cilantro (optional)

1. Prepare Spice Paste.

2. Combine sweet potatoes, broth, chickpeas, tomatoes, okra and Spice Paste in large saucepan. Bring to a boil over high heat. Reduce heat to low. Cover and simmer 15 minutes. Uncover; simmer 10 minutes or until vegetables are tender.

3. Meanwhile, prepare Yellow Couscous.

4. Serve stew with couscous and hot pepper sauce. Garnish with cilantro.

Makes 4 servings

Spice Paste

  6 cloves garlic, peeled
  1 teaspoon coarse salt
  2 teaspoons paprika
1½ teaspoons whole cumin seeds
  1 teaspoon black pepper
½ teaspoon ground ginger
½ teaspoon ground allspice
  1 tablespoon olive oil

Process garlic and salt in blender or small food processor until garlic is finely chopped. Add remaining seasonings. Process 15 seconds. While blender is running, pour oil through cover opening; process until mixture forms paste.

continued on page 40

Spicy African Chickpea and Sweet Potato Stew, continued

Yellow Couscous

     1 tablespoon olive oil
     5 green onions, sliced
 1⅔ cups water
     ¼ teaspoon ground turmeric *or* ⅛ teaspoon saffron threads
     ¼ teaspoon salt
     1 cup couscous

Heat oil in medium saucepan over medium heat. Add green onions; cook and stir 4 minutes. Add water, turmeric and salt. Bring to a boil; stir in couscous. Remove from heat. Cover; let stand 5 minutes.

Makes 3 cups

Fish & Chips

 ¾ cup all-purpose flour
 ½ cup flat beer or lemon-lime carbonated beverage
     Vegetable oil
     4 medium russet potatoes, each cut into 8 wedges
     Salt
     1 egg, separated
     1 pound cod fillets (about 6 to 8 small fillets)
     Malt vinegar and lemon wedges (optional)

1. Combine flour, beer and 2 teaspoons oil in small bowl. Cover; refrigerate 1 to 2 hours.

2. Pour 2 inches oil into large, heavy skillet. Heat over medium heat to 365°F. Add potato wedges in batches. (Do not crowd.) Fry potato wedges 4 to 6 minutes or until browned, turning once. (Allow temperature of oil to return to 365°F between batches.) Drain on paper towels; sprinkle lightly with salt. Reserve oil to fry fish.

3. Stir egg yolk into reserved flour mixture. Beat egg white in medium bowl with electric mixer at medium-high speed until soft peaks form. Fold egg white into flour mixture.

4. Return oil to 365°F. Dip fish pieces into batter in batches; fry 4 to 6 minutes or until batter is crispy and brown and fish begins to flake when tested with fork, turning once. (Allow temperature of oil to return to 365°F between batches.) Drain on paper towels. Serve immediately with potato wedges. Sprinkle with vinegar and serve with lemon wedges, if desired.

Makes 4 servings

Cheese and Potato Burritos

1 pound Yukon gold or red potatoes, cut into ½-inch pieces
1 cup (4 ounces) shredded pepper jack cheese
2 green onions, finely chopped
¾ teaspoon salt, divided
2 pounds plum tomatoes, halved and seeded
1 cup lightly packed fresh cilantro
1 jalapeño pepper,* seeded and coarsely chopped
¼ small red onion, coarsely chopped
1 clove garlic, quartered
¼ cup water
1 tablespoon fresh lime juice
¾ teaspoon ground cumin
12 (6-inch) flour tortillas
   Nonstick cooking spray

*Jalapeño peppers can sting and irritate the skin, so wear rubber gloves when handling peppers and do not touch your eyes.

1. Prepare grill for direct cooking.

2. Place potatoes in medium saucepan; cover halfway with water. Bring to a boil. Cover; cook over medium heat about 8 minutes or until tender. Drain; stir in cheese, green onions and ¼ teaspoon salt. Keep warm.

3. Meanwhile, grill tomatoes, skin-side down, on grid over medium-high heat about 5 minutes or until skin is blackened and tomatoes are very tender. Combine cilantro, jalapeño pepper, red onion and garlic in food processor; process using on/off pulsing action until finely chopped. Transfer to medium bowl. Place tomatoes, water, lime juice, cumin and remaining ½ teaspoon salt in food processor; process until smooth. Add to cilantro mixture.

4. Lightly spray tortillas on both sides with cooking spray; grill until warmed.

5. Top each tortilla with 1 tablespoon tomato sauce. Spoon potato mixture down centers; roll to enclose filling. Spoon remaining sauce over burritos.   *Makes 6 servings*

Note: Burritos are best served just after assembly. Store leftovers as separate components and assemble just before serving. Reheat in microwave.

Portuguese Potato & Greens Soup

2 tablespoons olive oil
1 cup chopped onion
1 cup chopped carrots
2 cloves garlic, minced
1 pound unpeeled new red potatoes, cut into 1-inch pieces
2 cups water
1 can (about 14 ounces) chicken broth
½ pound chorizo sausage, casings removed
½ pound kale
   Salt and black pepper

1. Heat oil in large saucepan over medium heat. Add onion, carrots and garlic; cook and stir 5 to 6 minutes or until lightly browned. Add potatoes, water and broth. Bring to a boil. Reduce heat to low. Cover; simmer 10 to 15 minutes or until potatoes are tender.

2. Meanwhile, heat large nonstick skillet over medium heat. Crumble chorizo into skillet. Cook and stir 5 to 6 minutes or until sausage is cooked through. Drain on paper towels.

3. Wash kale; remove tough stems. Slice into thin shreds.

4. Add sausage and kale to broth mixture; cook over medium heat 4 to 5 minutes or until heated through. Kale should be bright green and slightly crunchy. Season with salt and pepper.

Makes 4 servings

Tater Tip

Potatoes and greens are a classic combination wherever potatoes are grown. The English have Bubble and Squeak. The Irish enjoy Colcannon (see page 48 for a recipe). Feel free to choose your own favorite greens for these recipes. Chard, mustard greens, spinach and collards will all work well.

Potato Gnocchi with Tomato Sauce

   2 pounds baking potatoes (3 or 4 large)
⅔ to 1 cup all-purpose flour, divided
   1 egg yolk
½ teaspoon salt
⅛ teaspoon ground nutmeg (optional)
   1 jar (about 24 ounces) meatless pasta sauce
      Freshly grated Parmesan cheese
      Slivered fresh basil

1. Preheat oven to 425°F. Pierce potatoes several times with fork. Bake 1 hour or until soft.

2. Cut potatoes in half lengthwise; cool slightly. Scoop pulp from skins into medium bowl; discard skins. Mash potatoes until smooth. Add ⅓ cup flour, egg yolk, salt and nutmeg, if desired; mix well to form dough.

3. Turn out dough onto well-floured surface. Knead in enough remaining flour to form smooth dough that is not sticky. Divide dough into 4 equal portions. Roll each portion with hands on lightly floured surface into ¾- to 1-inch-wide rope. Cut each rope into 1-inch pieces; gently press thumb into center of each piece to make indentation. Transfer gnocchi to lightly floured kitchen towel in single layer to prevent sticking.

4. Bring 4 quarts salted water to a gentle boil in Dutch oven over medium-high heat. To test gnocchi cooking time, drop several into water; cook 1 minute or until they float to surface. Remove from water with slotted spoon and taste for doneness. (If gnocchi start to dissolve, shorten cooking time by several seconds.) Cook remaining gnocchi in batches, removing with slotted spoon to warm serving dish.

5. Meanwhile, warm pasta sauce in medium saucepan over low heat. Serve gnocchi with sauce; sprinkle with cheese and basil.   *Makes 4 servings*

Spanish Tortilla

1 teaspoon olive oil
1 cup thinly sliced red potatoes
1 small zucchini, thinly sliced
¼ cup chopped onion
1 clove garlic, minced
1 cup shredded cooked chicken
8 eggs
½ teaspoon salt
½ teaspoon black pepper
¼ teaspoon red pepper flakes
Fresh tomato salsa (optional)

1. Heat oil in large nonstick skillet over medium-high heat. Add potato, zucchini, onion and garlic; cook and stir about 5 minutes or until potato is tender, turning frequently. Stir in chicken; cook 1 minute.

2. Meanwhile, whisk eggs, salt, black pepper and red pepper flakes in large bowl. Carefully pour egg mixture into skillet. Reduce heat to low. Cover and cook 12 to 15 minutes or until egg mixture is set in center.

3. Loosen edges of tortilla and slide onto large serving platter. Let stand 5 minutes before cutting into wedges or 1-inch cubes. Serve warm or at room temperature. Serve with salsa, if desired.   *Makes 10 to 12 servings*

Tater Tip

This tortilla is not your typical tortilla used in Mexican cooking as a wrap for savory fillings. It is a Spanish omelet, or tortilla española, similar to an Italian frittata. It is traditionally made with potatoes, eggs and onions, but you can make any variety of tortilla as you would an omelet. It is excellent for all meals of the day or as a tapa, and it can be served warm, cool or at room temperature.

Pasta & Potatoes with Pesto

    3 medium red potatoes, cut into chunks
    8 ounces uncooked linguine
    ¾ cup frozen peas
    1 package (about 7 ounces) prepared pesto sauce
    ¼ cup plus 2 tablespoons grated Parmesan cheese, divided
    ¼ teaspoon salt
    ¼ teaspoon black pepper

1. Place potatoes in medium saucepan; cover with water. Bring to a boil over high heat; reduce heat. Cook, uncovered, 10 minutes or until potatoes are tender; drain.

2. Meanwhile, cook linguine according to package directions, adding peas during last 3 minutes of cooking; drain. Return pasta mixture to pan; add potatoes, pesto sauce, ¼ cup cheese, salt and pepper, tossing until blended.

3. Sprinkle with remaining 2 tablespoons cheese.   *Makes 6 servings*

Cabbage Colcannon

    1 pound new red potatoes, halved
    1 tablespoon vegetable oil
    1 small onion, thinly sliced
    ½ small head green cabbage, thinly sliced
        Salt and black pepper
    3 tablespoons salted butter

1. Place potatoes and enough water to cover in medium saucepan. Bring to a boil. Cook 20 minutes or until tender. Drain well.

2. Heat oil in large nonstick skillet over medium-high heat. Add onion; cook and stir 8 minutes or until onion is lightly browned. Add cabbage; cook and stir 5 minutes or until softened.

3. Add potatoes to skillet; cook until heated through. Slightly mash potatoes. Season to taste with salt and pepper. Place ½ tablespoon butter on each portion just before serving.   *Makes 6 servings*

Mashed, Fried & On the Side

Lemon-Mint Red Potatoes

2 pounds new red potatoes
3 tablespoons olive oil
1 teaspoon salt
¾ teaspoon Greek seasoning or dried oregano
¼ teaspoon garlic powder
¼ teaspoon black pepper
1 teaspoon grated lemon peel
2 tablespoons lemon juice
2 tablespoons butter
4 tablespoons chopped fresh mint, divided

Slow Cooker Directions

1. Coat inside of 6-quart slow cooker with nonstick cooking spray. Add potatoes and oil, stirring gently to coat. Sprinkle with salt, Greek seasoning, garlic powder and pepper. Cover; cook on LOW 7 hours or on HIGH 4 hours.

2. Stir in lemon peel, lemon juice, butter and 2 tablespoons mint until butter is completely melted. Cover; cook 15 minutes to allow flavors to blend. Sprinkle with remaining 2 tablespoons mint just before serving.

Makes 4 servings

Prep Time: 25 minutes
Cook Time: 7¼ hours (LOW) or 4¼ hours (HIGH)

Tip: Potatoes can stand, covered, at room temperature for up to 2 hours.

Creamy Golden Mushroom Mashed Potatoes

6 medium baking potatoes, cut into 1-inch pieces (about 6 cups)
1 small onion, cut into wedges
   Water
1 can (10¾ ounces) CAMPBELL'S® Condensed Golden Mushroom Soup
¾ cup milk
¼ cup heavy cream
4 tablespoons butter

1. Put the potatoes and onion in a 4-quart saucepot with enough water to cover them. Heat the potatoes over medium-high heat to a boil. Reduce the heat to low. Cover and cook the potatoes for 20 minutes or until they're fork-tender. Drain the potatoes and onion well in a colander.

2. Put the potatoes and onion in a 3-quart bowl and beat with an electric mixer at medium speed until almost smooth.

3. Put the soup, milk, cream and butter in a 4-cup microwavable measuring cup. Microwave on HIGH for 2½ minutes or until hot. Slowly pour the hot soup mixture into the potatoes, beating with an electric mixer at medium speed until the potatoes are smooth. Season to taste.

Makes 6 servings

Prep Time: 20 minutes
Cook Time: 30 minutes

Parmesan Potato Wedges

   2 pounds red potatoes, cut into ½-inch wedges
   ¼ cup finely chopped yellow onion
1½ teaspoons dried oregano
   ½ teaspoon salt
      Black pepper
   2 tablespoons butter, cut into small pieces
   ¼ cup grated Parmesan cheese

Slow Cooker Directions

Layer potatoes, onion, oregano, salt, pepper and butter in slow cooker. Cover; cook on HIGH 4 hours. Transfer potatoes to serving platter and sprinkle with cheese.

Makes 6 servings

Prep Time: 10 minutes
Cook Time: 4 hours (HIGH)

Peasant Potatoes

   ¼ cup (½ stick) butter
   1 large onion, chopped
   2 cloves garlic, chopped
   ½ pound smoked beef sausage, cut into ¾-inch slices
   1 teaspoon dried oregano
   6 medium Yukon Gold potatoes, cut into 2-inch pieces
      Salt and black pepper
   2 cups sliced savoy or other cabbage
   1 cup diced or sliced roasted red bell peppers
   ½ cup grated Parmesan cheese

Slow Cooker Directions

1. Melt butter in large skillet over medium heat. Add onion and garlic; cook and stir 5 minutes or until onion is translucent. Stir in sausage and oregano; cook 5 minutes. Stir in potatoes, salt and black pepper. Transfer mixture to slow cooker.

2. Cover; cook on LOW 6 to 8 hours or on HIGH 3 to 4 hours, stirring every hour. Add cabbage and bell peppers during last 30 minutes of cooking.

3. Top with Parmesan cheese before serving.

Makes 6 servings

Potato-Cauliflower Mash

    3 cups water
    2 cups cubed Yukon Gold potatoes
10 ounces frozen cauliflower florets
¼ cup half-and-half
    2 tablespoons butter
¾ teaspoon salt
¼ teaspoon black pepper

1. Bring water to a boil in large saucepan. Add potatoes and cauliflower and return to a boil. Reduce heat. Cover; simmer 10 minutes or until potatoes are tender.

2. Drain well. Return potatoes and cauliflower to saucepan. Add half-and-half, butter, salt and pepper; mash until smooth.

Makes 4 servings

Zippy Oven Fries

    1 pound russet potatoes, sliced into ¼-inch wedges
    3 tablespoons melted butter or vegetable oil
    2 tablespoons *Frank's® RedHot®* Original Cayenne Pepper Sauce, at room temperature
    2 cups *French's®* French Fried Onions, finely crushed
½ cup grated Parmesan cheese
    Zestup Ketchup (recipe follows)

1. Preheat oven to 400°F. Place potatoes, butter and *Frank's RedHot* Sauce in large resealable plastic bag. Seal bag and toss potatoes to coat.

2. Combine French Fried Onions and cheese on sheet of waxed paper. Coat potatoes in crumb mixture, pressing firmly.

3. Arrange potatoes in single layer in shallow baking pan coated with nonstick cooking spray. Bake, uncovered, 25 minutes or until potatoes are tender and golden brown. Splash on more *Frank's RedHot* Sauce or serve with Zestup Ketchup.

Makes 4 servings

Prep Time: 10 minutes
Cook Time: 25 minutes

Zestup Ketchup: Combine 1 cup ketchup with 1 to 2 tablespoons *Frank's RedHot* Sauce.

Vegetable Casserole

    2 packages (10 ounces each) frozen spinach
    ¾ cup (1½ sticks) butter, divided
        Salt and black pepper
    8 potatoes, peeled and cooked until tender
    1 cup milk
    1 pound carrots, sliced and cooked until tender
    1 pound green beans, cut into 1-inch pieces and cooked until tender
    ½ teaspoon paprika

1. Preheat oven to 375°F. Lightly grease 4-quart casserole or roasting pan.

2. Cook spinach according to package directions; drain and squeeze dry. Spread spinach in prepared casserole; dot with 1 tablespoon butter and season with salt and pepper.

3. Mash potatoes with milk and ½ cup butter in large bowl until creamy.

4. Layer half of potatoes, carrots and green beans over spinach. Dot with another 1 tablespoon butter; season with salt and pepper.

5. Top with remaining potatoes. Dot with remaining 2 tablespoons butter and sprinkle with paprika. Bake 1 hour or until heated through and lightly browned.

Makes 10 to 12 servings

Tater Tip

To peel potatoes, use a swivel-bladed vegetable peeler rather than a knife. The skin and the flesh below the skin are rich in vitamins, so peel away as little of the flesh as possible. Cut out the "eyes" and any blemishes or green spots. To quickly cook potatoes, cut them into small pieces. Place the potatoes and enough water to cover in a large saucepan and bring to a boil over high heat. Reduce the heat to medium and simmer until the potatoes are fork-tender. Drain.

Chunky Ranch Potatoes

  3 pounds medium red potatoes, quartered
  1 cup water
  ½ cup prepared ranch dressing
  ½ cup grated Parmesan or Cheddar cheese (optional)
  ¼ cup minced chives

Slow Cooker Directions

1. Place potatoes in 4-quart slow cooker. Add water. Cover; cook on LOW 7 to 9 hours or on HIGH 4 to 6 hours or until potatoes are tender.

2. Stir in ranch dressing, cheese, if desired, and chives. Break up potatoes into chunks.

Makes 8 servings

Prep Time: 10 minutes
Cook Time: 7 to 9 hours (LOW) or 4 to 6 hours (HIGH)

Garlic Fries

  1 envelope LIPTON® RECIPE SECRETS® Savory Herb with Garlic Soup Mix*
  1 cup plain dry bread crumbs
  2 pounds large red or all-purpose potatoes, cut lengthwise into wedges
  ⅓ cup I CAN'T BELIEVE IT'S NOT BUTTER!® Spread, melted

*Also terrific with LIPTON® RECIPE SECRETS® Onion Soup Mix.

1. Preheat oven to 400°F. In large bowl, blend soup mix with bread crumbs. Dip potatoes in I Can't Believe It's Not Butter!® Spread, then soup mixture, until evenly coated.

2. In 15½×10½×1-inch jelly-roll pan sprayed with nonstick cooking spray, arrange potatoes in single layer.

3. Bake uncovered 40 minutes or until potatoes are tender and golden brown.

Makes 4 servings

Mediterranean Red Potatoes

      3 medium red potatoes, cut into bite-size pieces
   ⅔ cup fresh or frozen pearl onions
         Garlic-flavored cooking spray
   ¾ teaspoon Italian seasoning
   ¼ teaspoon black pepper
   1 tomato, seeded and chopped
   2 ounces (½ cup) crumbled feta cheese
   2 tablespoons chopped black olives

Slow Cooker Directions

1. Place potatoes and onions in 1½-quart soufflé dish. Spray potatoes and onions with cooking spray; toss to coat. Add Italian seasoning and pepper; mix well. Cover dish tightly with foil.

2. Tear off 3 (18×3-inch) strips of heavy-duty foil. Cross strips to resemble wheel spokes. Place soufflé dish in center of strips. Pull foil strips up and over dish to make handles and place dish into slow cooker.

3. Pour hot water into slow cooker to about 1½ inches from top of soufflé dish. Cover; cook on LOW 7 to 8 hours.

4. Use foil handles to lift dish out of slow cooker. Stir tomato, feta cheese and olives into potato mixture.   *Makes 4 servings*

Rustic Garlic Mashed Potatoes

      2 pounds baking potatoes, cut into ½-inch cubes
   ¼ cup water
      2 tablespoons butter, cut into small pieces
   1¼ teaspoons salt
   ½ teaspoon garlic powder
   ¼ teaspoon black pepper
   1 cup milk

Slow Cooker Directions

Place all ingredients except milk in slow cooker; toss to combine. Cover; cook on LOW 7 hours or on HIGH 4 hours. Add milk; mash potatoes with potato masher or electric mixer until smooth.   *Makes 6 servings*

Baked Sweet Potato Fries with Spicy Apricot Dipping Sauce

3 large sweet potatoes, peeled and cut into narrow wedges
2 tablespoons vegetable oil
1½ teaspoons coarse or kosher salt
¼ teaspoon black pepper
    Spicy Apricot Dipping Sauce (recipe follows)

1. Heat oven to 450°F. Gently toss potatoes, oil, salt and pepper in large bowl until potatoes are evenly coated. Divide potatoes between two large cookie sheets or jelly-roll pans. Bake 30 minutes or until lightly browned.

2. Meanwhile, prepare Spicy Apricot Dipping Sauce. Serve with hot potatoes.

Makes 6 servings

Spicy Apricot Dipping Sauce

1 cup apricot jam
¼ cup orange juice
1 tablespoon prepared mustard
¼ teaspoon ground red pepper

Melt jam in small saucepan over medium-high heat. Whisk in orange juice, mustard and red pepper. Purée sauce in food processor or with immersion blender, if desired.

Makes 6 servings

Tip: This sauce can also be served with chicken, either as a dipping sauce, or brushed over cooked chicken and browned briefly under the broiler for a tasty glaze.

Stuffed, Baked & Roasted

Twice-Baked Potatoes with Sun-Dried Tomatoes

4 large baking potatoes
  Vegetable oil
1 container (16 ounces) sour cream
2 cups (8 ounces) shredded Cheddar cheese, divided
⅓ cup sun-dried tomatoes packed in oil, drained and chopped
4 tablespoons finely chopped green onions, divided
2 tablespoons butter, softened
1 teaspoon salt
½ teaspoon black pepper

1. Preheat oven to 350°F. Scrub potatoes and pat dry with paper towels. Rub potatoes with oil; pierce in several places with fork. Bake 1 hour. Cool 30 minutes.

2. Cut potatoes in half lengthwise. Scrape potato pulp into large bowl, leaving ½-inch-thick shells. Add sour cream, 1½ cups cheese, sun-dried tomatoes, 3 tablespoons green onions, butter, salt and pepper; mix gently. Spoon into potato shells.

3. Place potatoes on baking sheet. Bake 15 to 20 minutes or until heated through. Top with remaining ½ cup cheese; bake 5 minutes or until cheese is melted. Sprinkle with remaining 1 tablespoon green onion.

Makes 8 servings

Spinach and Potatoes au Gratin

4 large red potatoes, cut into ¼-inch-thick slices
2 bags (6 ounces each) baby spinach*
2 tablespoons butter, melted
¼ teaspoon salt
⅛ teaspoon black pepper
½ cup whipping cream
⅛ teaspoon ground nutmeg
½ cup grated Parmesan cheese

*You may substitute regular spinach, but remove tough stems after washing.

1. Preheat oven to 350°F. Grease 11×7-inch baking dish. Arrange half of potato slices in dish.

2. Bring large saucepan of water to a boil. Add spinach; cook 30 seconds or until wilted. Drain. Rinse under cold water; squeeze out excess moisture. Place half of spinach on potato slices. Drizzle with melted butter. Sprinkle with half of salt and pepper. Top with remaining potatoes and spinach. Sprinkle with remaining salt and pepper. Combine cream and nutmeg in small bowl; pour over spinach.

3. Bake 40 to 50 minutes or until potatoes are almost tender. Remove from oven; sprinkle with cheese. Bake 15 minutes or until cheese is lightly browned and potatoes are tender. If cheese browns too quickly, cover loosely with foil.   *Makes 6 servings*

Tip: To prepare ahead, bake 50 minutes or until the potatoes are tender. Cover and refrigerate up to one day. To serve, sprinkle with cheese and bake in a preheated 350°F oven 15 to 20 minutes or until heated through and the cheese is lightly browned.

Mexican Hash Brown Bake

    Nonstick cooking spray
    1 container (13 ounces) ORTEGA® Salsa & Cheese Bowl
1½ cups sour cream
    1 can (4 ounces) ORTEGA® Diced Green Chiles or Diced Jalapeños
    1 package (30 ounces) frozen shredded hash brown potatoes
    2 ORTEGA® Taco Shells, coarsely crushed

Preheat oven to 350°F. Spray 13×9-inch baking dish with cooking spray.

Combine Salsa & Cheese, sour cream and chiles in large bowl; stir until blended. Gently stir in hash browns. Spoon mixture into baking dish.

Sprinkle with crushed taco shells.

Bake for 45 to 50 minutes or until bubbly around edges. Let stand for 5 minutes before serving.
Makes 12 servings

Tip: Make this dish extra special by adding two sliced green onions or two slices crisp, crumbled bacon.

Thyme-Scented Roasted Sweet Potatoes and Onions

    2 large sweet potatoes (about 1¼ pounds)
    1 medium sweet or yellow onion, cut into chunks
    2 tablespoons canola oil
    1 teaspoon dried thyme
    ½ teaspoon salt
    ½ teaspoon smoked paprika
    ⅛ teaspoon ground red pepper (optional)

1. Preheat oven to 425°F. Coat 15×10-inch jelly-roll pan with nonstick cooking spray.

2. Cut sweet potatoes into 1-inch chunks; place in large bowl. Add onion, oil, thyme, salt, paprika and red pepper, if desired; toss well. Spread vegetables in single layer on prepared pan.

3. Bake 20 to 25 minutes or until very tender, stirring after 10 minutes. Let stand 5 minutes before serving.
Makes 10 servings

Gratin of Two Potatoes

2 large baking potatoes (about 1¼ pounds)
2 large sweet potatoes (about 1¼ pounds)
1 tablespoon unsalted butter
1 large onion, thinly sliced and separated into rings
2 teaspoons all-purpose flour
1 cup reduced-sodium chicken broth
½ teaspoon salt
¼ teaspoon white pepper *or* ⅛ teaspoon ground red pepper
¾ cup grated Parmesan cheese

1. Cook baking potatoes in large pot of boiling water 10 minutes. Add sweet potatoes; return to a boil. Simmer potatoes, uncovered, 25 minutes or until tender. Drain; cool under cold running water.

2. Meanwhile, melt butter in large nonstick skillet over medium-low heat. Add onion; cook 10 to 12 minutes or until tender, stirring occasionally. Sprinkle with flour; cook 1 minute, stirring frequently. Add broth, salt and pepper; bring to a boil over high heat. Reduce heat and simmer, uncovered, 2 minutes or until sauce thickens, stirring occasionally.

3. Preheat oven to 375°F. Spray 13×9-inch baking dish with nonstick cooking spray. Peel potatoes; cut crosswise into ¼-inch slices. Layer half of potato slices in prepared dish. Spoon half of onion mixture evenly over potatoes. Repeat layers. Cover with foil; bake 25 minutes or until heated through.

4. Preheat broiler. Uncover potatoes; sprinkle evenly with cheese. Broil, 5 inches from heat, 3 to 4 minutes or until cheese is bubbly and light golden brown.

Makes 6 servings

Roasted Peppers and Potatoes

2 pounds small red potatoes, quartered
1 large red bell pepper, cut into 1½-inch chunks
1 large yellow or orange bell pepper, cut into 1½-inch chunks
1 large red onion, cut into 1-inch pieces
¼ cup olive oil
3 cloves garlic, minced
¾ teaspoon salt
¼ teaspoon black pepper
¼ teaspoon dried basil
¼ teaspoon dried oregano

1. Preheat oven to 375°F.

2. Place potatoes, bell peppers and onion in large resealable food storage bag. Combine oil, garlic, salt, black pepper, basil and oregano in small bowl; pour over vegetables in bag. Seal; shake until vegetables are evenly coated. Spread on large baking sheet.

3. Bake 50 minutes or until potatoes are tender and beginning to brown, stirring every 15 minutes.
Makes 4 to 6 servings

Scalloped Potatoes with Gorgonzola

1 (14½-ounce) can chicken broth
1½ cups whipping cream
4 teaspoons minced garlic
1½ teaspoons dried sage leaves
1 cup BELGIOIOSO® Gorgonzola Cheese
2¼ pounds russet potatoes, peeled, halved and thinly sliced
Salt and pepper to taste

Preheat oven to 375°F. In medium heavy saucepan, simmer chicken broth, whipping cream, garlic and sage 5 minutes or until slightly thickened. Add BelGioioso® Gorgonzola Cheese and stir until melted. Remove from heat.

Place potatoes in large bowl and season with salt and pepper. Arrange half of potatoes in 13×9×2-inch glass baking dish. Pour half of cream mixture over top of potatoes. Repeat layers with remaining potatoes and cream mixture. Bake until potatoes are tender, about 1¼ hours. Let stand 15 minutes before serving.
Makes 8 servings

Taco-Topped Potatoes

4 red or Yukon gold potatoes (about 6 ounces each), scrubbed and pierced
    with fork
8 ounces ground beef
½ (1¼-ounce) package taco seasoning mix
½ cup water
1 cup diced tomatoes
¼ teaspoon salt
    Toppings: shredded lettuce, shredded sharp Cheddar cheese, finely chopped
    green onions and sour cream

1. Microwave potatoes on HIGH 6 to 7 minutes or until fork-tender.

2. Meanwhile, heat medium nonstick skillet over medium-high heat. Add beef and cook until browned, stirring to break up meat. Drain fat. Add seasoning mix and water; stir to blend. Cook 1 minute. Remove from heat.

3. Toss tomatoes with salt in medium bowl.

4. Split potatoes almost in half and fluff with fork. Fill with beef mixture. Top with tomatoes and desired toppings.

Makes 4 servings

Tater Tip

Don't scorn the skin! The skin of potatoes contains a lot of flavor and nutrients, so don't peel potatoes when you don't have to. Even if you plan to peel, cook potatoes with their skins, let them cool slightly and then peel. This will help the potatoes keep some of that good flavor and nutrition. When you know you are going to eat the skin, be sure to scrub them with a vegetable brush to get rid of embedded dirt. The skin and flesh of potatoes are a good source of fiber, vitamins and minerals, and are low in calories.

Scalloped Potato-Onion Bake

1 can (10¾ ounces) CAMPBELL'S® Condensed Cream of Celery Soup (Regular *or* 98% Fat Free)
½ cup milk
  Dash ground black pepper
4 medium potatoes (about 1¼ pounds), thinly sliced
1 small onion, thinly sliced (about ¼ cup)
1 tablespoon butter, cut into pieces
  Paprika

1. Stir the soup, milk and black pepper with a whisk or fork in a small bowl. Layer half of the potatoes, half of the onion and half of the soup mixture in a 1½-quart casserole. Repeat the layers. Place the butter over the soup mixture. Sprinkle with the paprika. Cover the dish with foil.

2. Bake at 400°F. for 1 hour. Uncover and bake for 15 minutes more or until the potatoes are fork-tender.   *Makes 6 servings*

Prep Time: 10 minutes
Bake Time: 1 hour 15 minutes

Bacon and Cheese Brunch Potatoes

3 medium russet potatoes (about 2 pounds), peeled and cut into 1-inch pieces
1 cup chopped onion
½ teaspoon seasoned salt
4 slices crisp-cooked and crumbled bacon
1 cup (4 ounces) shredded sharp Cheddar cheese
1 tablespoon water or chicken broth

Slow Cooker Directions

1. Coat slow cooker with nonstick cooking spray. Layer half of potatoes, onion, seasoned salt, bacon and cheese in slow cooker. Repeat layers, ending with cheese. Sprinkle water over top.

2. Cover; cook on LOW 6 hours or on HIGH 3½ hours or until potatoes and onion are tender. Stir gently to mix and serve hot.   *Makes 6 servings*

Prep Time: 10 minutes
Cook Time: 6 hours (LOW) or 3½ hours (HIGH)

Salads, Snacks & More

Garden Potato Salad with Basil-Yogurt Dressing

      6 new potatoes, quartered
      8 ounces asparagus, cut into 1-inch pieces
  1¼ cups red, yellow or green bell pepper strips
    ⅔ cup plain yogurt
    ¼ cup sliced green onions
      2 tablespoons chopped pitted ripe olives
  1½ tablespoons chopped fresh basil *or* 1½ teaspoons dried basil
      1 tablespoon chopped fresh thyme *or* 1 teaspoon dried thyme
      1 tablespoon white vinegar
      2 teaspoons sugar
         Dash ground red pepper

1. Bring 3 cups water to a boil in large saucepan over high heat. Add potatoes; return to a boil. Reduce heat to medium-low. Simmer, covered, 8 minutes. Add asparagus and bell peppers; return to a boil over high heat. Reduce heat to medium-low. Simmer, covered, about 3 minutes or until potatoes are just tender and asparagus and bell peppers are crisp-tender. Drain.

2. Meanwhile, combine yogurt, green onions, olives, basil, thyme, vinegar, sugar and ground red pepper in large bowl. Add vegetables; toss to combine. Refrigerate, covered, until well chilled.
Makes 4 servings

Sweet Potato & Fruit Salad

2 sweet potatoes (about 1¼ pounds)
1 small Granny Smith apple, unpeeled and chopped
¼ cup chopped celery
1 container (6 ounces) plain yogurt
2 tablespoons orange juice
½ to 1 teaspoon grated fresh ginger
½ teaspoon curry powder
⅛ teaspoon salt
½ cup cinnamon-coated nuts, divided
¼ cup drained mandarin oranges

1. Pierce sweet potatoes in several places with fork and place on microwavable dish. Cover loosely with microwave-safe plastic wrap. Microwave on HIGH 6 to 7 minutes, turning over halfway through cooking time. Cool completely.

2. Peel potatoes and cut into 1-inch pieces. Combine potatoes, apple and celery in large serving dish.

3. Combine yogurt, orange juice, ginger, curry powder and salt in small bowl. Stir into potato mixture. Add half of nuts; stir gently. Top with remaining nuts and oranges. Refrigerate until ready to serve. *Makes 4 to 6 servings*

Variations: Choose any type of roasted nut, including honey- or praline-coated. Add some chopped jalapeño pepper to spice it up.

Mini New Potato Bites

1½ pounds new potatoes (about 15 potatoes)
4 ounces (½ of 8-ounce package) PHILADELPHIA® Cream Cheese, softened
2 tablespoons BREAKSTONE'S® or KNUDSEN® Sour Cream
2 tablespoons KRAFT® 100% Grated Parmesan Cheese
4 slices OSCAR MAYER® Bacon, cooked, crumbled
2 tablespoons snipped fresh chives

PLACE potatoes in large saucepan; add enough water to cover. Bring to boil. Reduce heat to medium-low; cook 15 minutes or until potatoes are tender.

MIX cream cheese, sour cream and Parmesan cheese; cover. Refrigerate until ready to use.

DRAIN potatoes. Cool slightly. Cut potatoes in half; cut small piece from bottom of each potato half so potato lies flat. Place on serving platter. Top each potato half with 1 teaspoon of the cream cheese mixture. Sprinkle with bacon and chives.

Makes 15 servings, 2 topped potato halves each.

Prep Time: 30 minutes plus refrigerating

Make Ahead: These potatoes are delicious served hot or cold.

Substitution: Substitute PHILADELPHIA Chive & Onion Cream Cheese Spread for the regular cream cheese for added flavor.

Herbed Potato Chips

Nonstick olive oil cooking spray
2 medium red potatoes (about ½ pound)
1 tablespoon olive oil
2 tablespoons minced fresh dill, thyme or rosemary leaves
¼ teaspoon garlic salt
⅛ teaspoon black pepper

1. Preheat oven to 450°F. Spray baking sheets with cooking spray.

2. Cut potatoes crosswise into very thin slices, about 1/16 inch thick. Pat dry with paper towels. Arrange potato slices in single layer on prepared baking sheets; coat potatoes with cooking spray.

3. Bake 10 minutes; turn slices over. Brush with olive oil. Combine dill, garlic salt and pepper in small bowl; sprinkle evenly onto potato slices. Bake 5 to 10 minutes or until potatoes are golden brown. Cool on baking sheets. *Makes 6 servings*

Traditional German Potato Salad

2½ pounds red potatoes
¼ pound bacon, cut into small pieces
½ medium onion, finely chopped
½ cup cider vinegar
¼ cup water
1 tablespoon plus 1 teaspoon sugar
1 teaspoon salt
1 teaspoon brown mustard seeds
1 teaspoon mustard
2 tablespoons finely chopped fresh parsley
1 teaspoon paprika

1. Place potatoes in large saucepan. Add enough water to cover. Bring to a boil over high heat. Reduce heat and simmer, uncovered, 20 to 30 minutes or until potatoes are fork-tender. Drain; cool.

2. Cook bacon in medium skillet over medium heat until crisp. Remove with slotted spoon. Crumble into large bowl; set aside. Drain all but 3 tablespoons drippings from skillet.

3. For dressing, cook and stir onion in skillet until tender. Remove from heat. Combine vinegar, water, sugar, salt, mustard seeds and mustard in skillet. Keep warm.

4. Peel potatoes and cut into ¼-inch slices. Add potatoes to bowl with bacon. Pour warm dressing over potato mixture; toss to coat evenly. Sprinkle with parsley and paprika. Serve hot or cold.   *Makes 6 to 8 servings*

Note: This salad contains no eggs or mayonnaise and will keep well for picnics and other outdoor meals.

Thick Potato Chips with Beer Ketchup

Beer Ketchup (recipe follows)
1 quart peanut oil
3 baking potatoes, scrubbed
Sea salt and black pepper

1. Prepare Beer Ketchup. Heat oil in deep pan (oil should come up sides at least 3 inches) to 345°F.

2. Slice potatoes into ¼-inch-thick slices. Lower into oil in batches. Fry 2 to 3 minutes per side, flipping to brown evenly on both sides. Drain on paper towels and immediately sprinkle with salt and pepper.

3. Serve with Beer Ketchup.

Makes 4 servings

Tip: If the potatoes begin browning too quickly, turn down the heat and wait for the oil to cool to the proper temperature. Too high a temperature will not cook the potatoes completely, and too low a temperature will make the chips soggy.

Beer Ketchup

¾ cup ketchup
¼ cup beer
1 tablespoon Worcestershire sauce
¼ teaspoon onion powder
Ground red pepper

Mix all ingredients in small saucepan. Bring to a boil. Reduce heat; simmer 2 to 3 minutes. Remove from heat and let cool. Cover; refrigerate until ready to use.

Makes about 1 cup

Grilled Potato Salad

Dressing
- 4 tablespoons country-style Dijon mustard
- 3 tablespoons olive oil
- 2 tablespoons chopped fresh dill
- 1 tablespoon white wine or apple cider vinegar
- ½ teaspoon salt
- ¼ teaspoon black pepper

Salad
- 1 teaspoon salt
- 2 pounds small red potatoes, cut into ½-inch slices
- 2 tablespoons olive oil
- 1 green onion, thinly sliced

1. Combine all dressing ingredients in small jar with tight-fitting lid. Set aside.

2. Prepare grill for direct cooking. Fill large saucepan three-fourths full with water. Add 1 teaspoon salt and bring to a boil over high heat. Add potatoes; boil 5 minutes. Drain; return potatoes to saucepan. Drizzle with 2 tablespoons oil; toss lightly.

3. Spray 1 side of large sheet of foil with nonstick cooking spray. Transfer potatoes to foil; fold into packet. Place potato packet on grid over medium-high heat. Grill 7 to 10 minutes or until potatoes are tender. Transfer potatoes to serving bowl. Sprinkle with green onion. Shake dressing to combine. Pour over potatoes; toss gently. Serve warm.

Makes 4 servings

Tater Tip

There is a world of potatoes beyond the basic russet, white and red varieties. Fingerlings, a type of heritage potato that is small and shaped like a finger, are becoming more widely available at large supermarkets and farmers' markets. Search your local market from late summer to early winter for interesting and unusual colors of fingerlings, ranging from buttery yellow to deep fuchsia to vibrant blue and purple.

Tex-Mex Potato Skins

3 hot baked potatoes, split lengthwise
¾ cup (3 ounces) shredded Cheddar or pepper Jack cheese
1⅓ cups *French's®* French Fried Onions, divided
¼ cup chopped green chilies
¼ cup crumbled cooked bacon
Salsa and sour cream

1. Preheat oven to 350°F. Scoop out inside of potatoes, leaving ¼-inch shells. Reserve inside of potatoes for another use.

2. Arrange potato halves on baking sheet. Top with cheese, ⅔ cup French Fried Onions, chilies and bacon.

3. Bake 15 minutes or until heated through and cheese is melted. Cut each potato half crosswise into thirds. Serve topped with salsa, sour cream and remaining onions.

Makes 18 appetizer servings

Prep Time: 15 minutes
Cook Time: 15 minutes

Tip: To bake potatoes quickly, microwave at HIGH 10 to 12 minutes or until tender.

Variation: For added Cheddar flavor, substitute *French's®* Cheddar French Fried Onions for the original flavor.

Vegetable Potato Salad

1 envelope LIPTON® RECIPE SECRETS® Vegetable Soup Mix
1 cup HELLMANN'S® or BEST FOODS® Real Mayonnaise
2 teaspoons white vinegar
2 pounds red or all-purpose potatoes, cooked and cut into chunks
¼ cup finely chopped red onion (optional)

1. In large bowl, combine soup mix, mayonnaise and vinegar.

2. Add potatoes and onion; toss well. Chill 2 hours.

Makes 6 servings

Prep Time: 20 minutes
Chill Time: 2 hours

Acknowledgments

The publisher would like to thank the companies listed below
for the use of their recipes and photographs in this publication.

BelGioioso® Cheese Inc.

Campbell Soup Company

©2009 Kraft Foods, KRAFT, KRAFT Hexagon Logo, PHILADELPHIA AND PHILADELPHIA Logo
are registered trademarks of Kraft Foods Holdings, Inc. All rights reserved.

Ortega®, A Division of B&G Foods, Inc.

Reckitt Benckiser Inc.

Unilever